THE COMPLETE SOUP MAKER RECIPE BOOK

Quick and Healthy Recipes for The Whole Family incl. Low Carb Bonus

Olivia K. Evans

Copyright © 2020 by Olivia K. Evans

All rights reserved

All rights for this book here presented belong exclusively to the author.
Usage or reproduction of the text is forbidden and requires a clear consent of the author in case of expectations.

ISBN - 9781658655491

TABLE OF CONTENTS

Introduction 7
    The History Of Soup Creation 7
    Weight Loss With The Use Of Soup Meals 8
    Types of weight soups for weight loss 8
    What do I need for cooking soups 11

Recipes 13
    Classical Soups Recipes 15
        Classic Tomato Soup Recipe 16
        Classical Swiss and French Squash Soup 17
        Classic Chicken Noodle Soup 18
        Classic Vichyssoise Soup 20
        Classic French Onion Soup 22
        Avgolemono: Greek Lemon Chicken Soup 24
        Classic Fish Soup 26
        Minestrone Soup with Chicken 28
        Grandma's Chicken 'n' Dumpling Soup 30
        Fresh Corn & Potato Chowder 32
    Soups With Meat Recipes 33
        Vegetable Beef Soup 34
        Steak Soup 36
        Hearty Beef Soup 38
        Chicken Easy Crock Pot Meatball Soup 40
        Simple Chicken Soup 41
        The Ultimate Chicken Noodle Soup 43
        Southwestern Pork Soup 45

TABLE OF CONTENTS

- Vegetable Pork Soup 47
- Soup Maker Turkey & Ham Cream Soup 48
- Bolognese Beef Soup 49

Soup with Fish Recipes 51
- Fish and Vegetable Soup 52
- Sicilian fish soup 53
- Fish Chowder Soup 55
- Easy Italian Fish Soup 57
- Umbrian Fish Soup 59
- Sopa de Pescado 61
- Fish soup for winter dinners 62
- Mediterranean Fish Soup 64
- Spicy fish soup 65
- Quick Easy Fish Stew 66

Cream Soup Recipes 69
- Creamy Chicken and Mushroom Soup 70
- Quick Cream of Mushroom Soup 72
- Homemade Creamy Vegetable Soup 73
- Creamy Chicken Soup 74
- BEST Homemade Cream of Celery Soup 76
- Quick and Easy Creamy Vegetable Soup 77
- Cream of tomato soup recipe 78
- Cream Soup Base 79
- Creamy Roasted Cauliflower Soup 80
- Creamy Potato Soup 82

TABLE OF CONTENTS

Vegetarian Soup Recipes 83
- Vegetarian Tortilla Soup 84
- Vegetable Tortellini Soup 86
- Greek Eat Your Greens Slimming World Speed Soup 87
- Soup Maker Lentil Soup 89
- Portuguese Green Bean & Carrot Soup 90
- Deconstructed Salad Soup 91
- Healthy Green Soup 92
- Minted Pea Soup 93
- Cream Of Broccoli Soup 94
- The Ultimate Leftover Vegan Soup 95

National Cuisine Soup Recipes 97
- Chinese chicken and sweetcorn Soup 98
- French Onion Soup 99
- The Ultimate Mediterranean Vegetable Soup 100
- Creamy Moroccan Carrot Soup 101
- Thai Vegetable Curry 102
- Portuguese Fish Soup 103
- Easy Indian Prawn Soup 104
- Gazpacho 105
- Chinese Easy Hot and Sour Soup 106
- Italian Wedding Soup 107

Disclaimer 108

INTRODUCTION

According to food historians, soups have probably existed for as long as cooked food has existed. The idea of combining ingredients to create a nutritious and easily digested food that was quite simple to serve was most likely among the earliest forms of cooked food that man ate. Evidence for the existence of soups can be traced to as far back in history as 20,000 BC. Although boiling food over heat only became widespread with the invention of clay vessels, early soups were most likely prepared in animal hides or waterproof baskets with hot rocks used to bring the water to boil.

Simple preparation and easy digestibility were some of the factors that inevitably favored the advancement of soups. It was recommended for invalids in ancient times. It was also the perfect food choice for traveling cultures.

Soup existed in various forms across different cultures all over the world. The Russian Borscht, Chinese Won Ton, Gazpacho in Spain and the French onion soup are all classic soups from different countries of the world. The word restaurant used to describe food establishments all over the world today has its roots from the French word for soup (soupe). It was first used to refer to highly concentrated soup in France back in the 16th century which was sold as a quick antidote for physical exhaustion. The word would, later on, be adopted as a description for food establishments that sold such soups after a shop specializing in "soups" was opened in France in 1765.

Several ancient cookbooks and other food literature from various regions of the world have also referred soups. A 1742 cookbook by William Parks included several bisques and soups recipes. Another cookbook Titled Frugal Housewife published in 1772 also has an entire chapter that described soups and how they can be prepared. The first full cooking pamphlet that was dedicated entirely to soup recipes was published by Emma Ewing in 1882.

The invention of canning as a method of food preservation in the 19th century has aided the popularity of commercial soups. Today, there are several canned soups on sale. However, the earliest forms of soups most likely only contained cereals that were roasted then ground before being made into a paste by adding water. Soups prepared for invalids were typically made of beaten eggs, cereals and legumes, and water extracted from boiling vegetables and other foods. Medicinal herbs and spices might have been added as well. Today, there are several possible combinations of ingredients used to make soups and a wide range of culinary preparations for them as well.

The concept of using a soup diet for weight loss has been around for several decades. While testimonies of users and several studies have shown that soup meals can indeed aid weight-loss, experts say that an all-soup diet may not be entirely sustainable mainly because it is lacking in all the nutrients needed for health and sustenance. Thus, it is generally agreed that eating soups packed with veggies as part of your weight loss plan is indeed a smart choice.

From research, it has been proven that eating soup increases satiety. By eating less, you can control your overall diet leading to weight loss. Regular soup intake has been associated with a low body max index. It is also believed that taking soup may help reduce waist circumference among other weight loss goals.

The earliest soup diet aimed specifically at inducing weight loss was the cabbage soup recipe which gained popularity in the 80s. at the time, it was believed that living on a cabbage soup recipe for one week could help you lose up to 10 lbs/4.5 kg. Over the years, variations of this recipe and many other soup-based plans for weight loss have been developed all with a promise of significant weight-loss within a short period. Some of these soup-diet plans include.

> **The basic soup diet:** on this plan, any type of soup is allowed from broth-based soups to creamy ones or meaty soups. Basic soup diets

typically span for 7 days other some may last for as long as 2 weeks with the promise of losing between 10-15 pounds if followed.

- **Cabbage soup diet:** this is the earliest form of soup-based diet for weight loss. Today, a cabbage soup diet includes different soup recipes with cabbage as the main ingredient. Most plans last up to 1 week with a promise of losing 10lbs. Most cabbage soup plans allow a restricted list of other foods that can be included and a long list of food that must be avoided.

- **Sacred heart diet:** this is a meat-based soup plan. This diet includes different soups with beef or chicken broth as the main ingredients. Other ingredients usually included include celery, tomatoes, carrots, onions, and green beans. On this plan, you may also eat other food such as brown rice, unsweetened fruit juice and so on with some other foods such as tomatoes and potatoes restricted to some specific days and in a measured amount. The sacred heart soup plan promises weight loss of between 10-17 lbs if followed strictly.

- **Bean soup plan:** this is another popular soup-based diet for weight loss. The bean soup diet includes ingredients such as mushrooms, diced tomatoes, chili peppers, pinto beans and celery as the core components. The plan involves eating bean soup as two main meals of the day. Plenty of water is recommended and food items like fruits, seeds, avocados, and nuts should be avoided. It is uncertain how much weight loss those who follow this plan can expect to achieve although several people claim it is quite effective as well.

- **Keto soup diet:** the Keto soup diet lasts for 5 days and promises a daily calorie intake of 1200 to 1400 calories per day. Those on a paleo diet or any other low-carb eating program can adopt a keto soup diet. It typically lasts for five days. Some of the popular ingredients included in the diet are bacon, tomatoes, red wine, green beans, squash, olive oil and so on.

While there are several variants of a soup diet for weight loss, there are some food trends that seem to be common to all. In most cases, compliant foods include:

- Chicken, beef or vegetable broth

- Green veggies like celery and green beans

- Tomatoes

Generally, those on a soup based weight loss diet are advised to avoid:

- Sweet treats e.g. Ice cream, candy, etc.

- Heavily processed snacks like crackers and chips.

- Diary products.

Most soup-based diets require you to add soup to every meal of the day including breakfast. However, some plans allow the freedom of one soup-free mals and two made up solely of soup with no snacking at all in-between. Soup weight loss diets can be modified to meet the needs of specific users. For example, users that need to cut down on sodium intake due to health conditions like hypertension may choose a plan that includes soups that have low sodium content or use low sodium ingredients.

If there is an argument against the use of soup diet for weight loss, it is the fact that is not sustainable. Like most mono-diets, you cannot live entirely on a soup diet. This is most likely why most plans last for 10 days or even less. Also, while weight-loss from a strict soup diet is quite substantial, it will most likely be from water loss rather than fat loss.

On the flip side, one of the advantages of a soup diet is over most other weight loss plan is the fact that you can still maintain your daily calorie intake without having to cut it down drastically. Some plans allow you to consume as much as 1400 calories daily which is a safe and reasonable calorie goal for anyone trying to lose weight healthily. However, bear in mind that since calorie requirement varies from one user to the other you should speak to a professional dietitian and consult your physician before embarking on any weight loss regimen.

Technically, you need nothing more than a pot and spoon to prepare soups. However, everyone knows that cooking is faster and a lot more convenient when you have the right utensils. You can cook more in less time than you would normally use and cook better quality soups with the right equipment. Below is a list of some of the kitchen items recommended for cooking soups:

1. Stockpot: a stockpot is essentially a pot, but it is larger and taller. The fact that it has a tall side is the biggest advantage here as it can hold a large quantity of liquid. It also helps to keep as much liquid as possible in the pot soup by minimizing evaporation and reduce spillage as the soup boils

2. China cap strainer: this is larger than your regular sieve. A china cap strainer is has a very fine mesh and is a lot deeper compared to regular colanders. This means it can allow you to pour in more soup to strain out unwanted parts for smoother soups.

3. Soup maker: the most modern way to prepare soups is by using a soup maker. A soup maker as the name implies helps to make soups in the simplest and fastest way possible. It is essentially a kettle-shaped unit with a glass or stainless steel body that has a heater at its base. Usually, a soup maker would have a lid with a motorized blade attached to it. When the unit is switched on, the heater at the base heats up and the blade spins (speed depends on selected setting); automatically preparing the soup.

   Based on the design of this appliance it is easy to see why it is the ultimate tool in your arsenal if you enjoy making soups. It is essentially a blender, pot, and cooker built into one appliance. You simply add in your ingredients, pick a setting and turn the appliance on. You can carry on with everything else you are doing as the soup maker has a timer that turns off the unit automatically (usually about 20-30 minutes based on the settings selected).

4. Food processor/blender: this is the closest alternative to a soupmaker for those who do not have one. It helps to grind soup mixtures to create smooth soups. Alternatively, you could also use an immersion blender. The advantage of this is that you do not have to risk transferring hot liquid from pot to blender and vice-versa.

Other important appliances and utensils for cooking soups include

- Storage containers-for storing or transporting food.

- Large pot/dutch oven- serve a similar purpose as a stockpot

- Soup skimmer- a flat circular strainer used for removing unwanted bits from the surface of your soup

- Long handle spoon (wooden)-for stirring soup without scraping the pot

- Ladle-for serving soup into bowls.

- Microplane or graters- for grating ingredients like ginger, garlic, nutmeg, etc for soup

- Slow cooker: fore preparing soups and tenderizing particularly tough ingredients such as root vegetables (e.g. potatoes) beans, tough meat cuts, etc.

- Thermos: for keeping portions of the soup at the desired temperature.

RECIPES

CLASSICAL SOUPS RECIPES

CLASSICAL SOUPS RECIPES

CLASSIC TOMATO SOUP RECIPE

Time: 1 hour

Amount: 8 servings

INGREDIENTS:

- 1 Finely chopped white onion
- Olive oil (2 tbsp)
- Unsalted butter (1 tbsp)
- All-purpose flour (2 tbsp)
- Smashed & peeled garlic clove (1 large)
- Peeled Whole plum tomatoes (1 28-oz can)- pureed
- chicken broth (3c)
- Sugar (1.5 tsp)
- Fresh thyme (1 sprig)
- Kosher salt
- Ground pepper (freshly ground)
- Fresh basil (thinly sliced) 3 tbsp (you can also use chives or dill)

HOW TO PREPARE

1. Heat oil & butter until the butter melts

2. Add onion & garlic to melted butter and sweat for 8 minutes. Stir occasionally as you cook until onions & garlic are softened.

3. Add broth, sugar, thyme, tomatoes, sauted onions and garlic into a soup maker & cook for 28 minutes. Remove and discard thyme sprig.

4. Set aside to cool for a while. Add salt & pepper to taste then reheat if necessary.

5. To be served warm (not hot) garnished with herbs

Time: 1 hour

Amount: 1 Serving

INGREDIENTS:

- Skim milk (1)
- Butter
- Salt
- Nutmeg
- Pepper
- 1 onion (peeled and minced)
- Squash (peeled and cubed)

HOW TO PREPARE:

1. Fry onions in the butter until it turns translucent

2. Add fried onions, squash, salt and milk into soup maker then cook on a smooth setting.

3. Add pepper and nutmeg to season and serve

CLASSIC CHICKEN NOODLE SOUP

Time: 3 hours

Amount: serves 6

INGREDIENTS

- 1 chicken and neck (3 lbs/1.35kg)
- Water (3 1/2 quarts)
- Carrots (2-coarsely chopped & 2 sliced)
- Celery ribs (2-coarsely chopped and 2 thinly-sliced (1/4 inch thick)
- Thick onion (1, unpeeled)
- 1 large Garlic clove (quartered and unpeeled)
- Smashed whole black peppercorns (1tsp)
- 1 Fresh bay leaf (large)
- Parsely sprigs (6)
- Thyme sprigs (1)
- Kosher salt
- Thing egg noodles (1/2 pounds or 0.27kg)
- Finely chopped flat-leaf parsley (1/4 cup)

HOW TO PREPARE

1. Mix chicken and neck, chopped celery & carrot, onions, garlic, herbs, peppercorns and water in stockpot then bring to boil.

2. Cover partially then simmer briefly (30 minutes). Remove the chicken from pot and place on a plate.

3. Discard chicken skin and pull meat off the bones then chop into small pieces 1/2 inches thick. Keep aside in a refrigerator

CLASSIC CHICKEN NOODLE SOUP

4. Return chicken bones to pot, cook on simmering heat for about an hour, strain broth then aside.

5. Transfer broth to soup maker. Add sliced carrots, celery, & seasoning cover and switch soup maker on. Cook for about 15 minutes on smooth or chunky setting as desired.

6. Cook noddles in boiling water. Drain, cool under cold running water.

7. Add the soup along with noodles, parsley and the chicken earlier set aside in a large pot & bring to simmer. To be served hot.

CLASSIC VICHYSSOISE SOUP

Time: 1 hr 45minutes

Amount: 4 (main course) or 6 (appetizer)

INGREDIENTS:

- 1 large onion (chopped)
- Butter (2 tbsp)
- Potatoes (3 large, peeled & diced)
- 6 leeks (rinsed and sliced)
- Olive oil (1 tbsp)
- Chicken broth (1quart/4 cup)
- Nutmeg (a pinch)
- Salt & pepper (to taste)
- Heavy cream (1/2 cup)
- Chives

HOW TO COOK:

1. In a pot or saucepan heat olive oil and butter on medium to high setting

2. Add onions and saute for about 2 minutes until onions become translucent.

3. Add leeks and cook for 5 minutes or less until it is soft.

4. Add in potatoes and cook for a couple of minutes more. Season with salt & pepper.

5. Pour sauted vegetables and chicken broth into soup maker & cook for about 25 minutes in smooth or chunky mode.

6 Add some heavy cream then turn soup maker back on. Cook for 5 minutes and turn off again. Add nutmeg to season.

7 Set soup aside and leave for an hour or more until it cools down to room temperature

8 Serve chilled, garnished with some chives.

CLASSIC FRENCH ONION SOUP

Time: 2 hours

Amount: Serves 12

INGREDIENTS:

- Oil (5 tbsp, divided)-preferably olive oil
- Sliced onions (8 cups)
- Butter (1 tbsp)
- Garlic(3 cloves, minced)
- Garlic cloves (2-large, halved and peeled)
- Port wine (1/2 c)
- Beef or vegetable broth (2 cartons, about 32oz/907g each)
- Salt (1/4 tsp)
- Pepper (1/2 tsp)
- Swiss cheese or shredded Gruyere (3/4 cup)
- Sliced fresh bread baguette (24, 1/2" thick)

HOW TO PREPARE

1. In a pot or suacepan, heat olive oil and some butter then add onions

2. Cook onion in oil until softened and it starts to turn golden brown. Stir while you cook.

3. Transfer onions to soup maker. Add in the garlic & stir in the wine. Pour sauted ingredients along with broth, pepper & salt then cook for 25 minutes on smooth or chunky setting based on what you prefer.

4 Place baguette slices on baking sheet the bake for some minutes in preheated oven. Prepare baguette by brushing both sides of it with oil. Bake for 3-5 minutes on both sides until it it toasted then rub toasts with the halved garlic

5 Serve in broiler safe bowl or ramekins on baking sheet. Place 2 toasts in each bowl along with soup. Top with choose and broil for a while to melt cheese before serving.

CLASSIC FRENCH ONION SOUP

AVGOLEMONO: GREEK LEMON CHICKEN SOUP

Time: 35 minutes

Amount: 6 servings

INGREDIENTS

- Extra virgin olive oil
- Carrots-finely chopped (1/2-1 cup)
- Celery-finely chopped (1/2 to 1 cup)
- Green onions-finely chopped (1/2 to 1 cup)
- Finely chopped garlic cloves (2)
- Chicken broth (low sodium)-8 cups
- Bay leaves-2
- Rice (1 cup)
- 2 Cooked chicken breast (boneless, shredded)
- Lemon juice- (1/2 cup, freshly squeezed)
- Eggs- (2 large)
- Freshly parsley (for garnish)-optional

HOW TO COOK

1. Heat olive oil in a heavy pot or dutch oven. To this, add celery, carrots and green onions. Toss and sauce briefly. Add in garlic

2. Add the chicken broth and the bay leaves to soup maker. Add rice, pepper & salt then turn soup maker on on cook for 25 minutes on smooth setting.

3. To prepare egg-lemon sauce, whisk eggs & lemon juice in a bowl. To this, add some broth from the cooking pot (add about 2 ladles).

4 Once fully mixed, add sauce to the chicken soup then stir. Remove from heat immediately

5 To be served hot, garnished with parsley and served with fresh bread.

CLASSIC FISH SOUP

Time: 1hrs 30 mins
Amount: 12 servings

INGREDIENTS

- Onions (6)
- Garlic (1 head)
- Olive oil
- Fennel bulb (1, fresh)
- Leeks (1 bunch)
- Celery (1 stick)
- Tomato paste (50g)
- Fish bones & trimmings (4 kg/8.8lbs)
- Cayanne pepper
- Salt
- Bouquet garni (1 large)
- Saffron
- Fennel seeds (1 handful)
- Pepper
- Water (10 liters)

For garnish:

- Baguette (1)
- Garlic cloves (2)
- Rouille sauce
- Emmental cheese or Grated Gruyere

HOW TO COOK

1. Peel and slice onions then sweat in olive oil. Stir regularly to prevent onions from sticking to the pan.

2. Add coarsely sliced leeks and celery, garlic head (cut in half) and the fennel bulb (thinly sliced) and mix well.

3. Crush fish bones & add this to the vegetables. Sweat while stirring regularly. Add the tomato paste, fennel seeds and bouquet garni.

4. Transfer ingredients to a soup maker, add some water until ingredients are fully immersed, then add salt, pepper & Espellete pepper to season. Cover & cook in soup maker for about 30 minutes

5. Meanwhile, rub some garlic on baguette then cut into slices about 0.5 cm thick. Place the bread slices on oven rack. Grill in an oven or salamander

6. When the fish mixture is cooked. Press as firmly as possible to extract juice. Discard the remaining bones. Repeat is the same for the remaining soup until a thick juice is formed.

7. Add saffron then season to taste if needed. To be served hot with grated cheese, garlic croutons with a side of rouille sauce.

MINESTRONE SOUP WITH CHICKEN

Time: 40 minutes

Amount: 10 servings

INGREDIENTS

- Olive oil (2 teaspoons)
- Sliced celery (2 stalks)
- Carrots-peeled & sliced (2, medium)
- Onion-diced (1, medium)
- Garlic cloves-chopped (2, medium)
- Chicken stock (or vegetable stock) -7 cups
- Italian seasoning (2 tsp)
- Red kidney beans-rinsed then drained (15 oz/425g can)
- chickpeas beans-rinsed then drained (15 oz/425can)
- Canned Tomatoes with juice (14 oz/400g can)
- Zucchini-chopped (1, medium)
- Uncooked macaroni (or any other short pasta)-1 cup
- Salt (1 tsp)
- Shredded chicken-cooked (2 cups)
- Pepper (1/2 tsp)
- Parmesan cheese-grated (1/2 cup)

HOW TO MAKE

1. In a sauce pot or stock pot, heat oil over medium to high heat

2. Add onions, celery and carrots then cook for 5 minutes or less until softened

3. Add in garlic and stir

4. Add the chicken stock/vegetable stock, beans, chickpeas, tomatoes and italian seasoning into soup maker. Also, transfer sauted ingredients into soup maker & cook for about 25 minutes.

5. Return the soup to a pot. Add pasta, chicken and zucchini. Add half of the salt to season then taste (add more if required). Add pepper.

6. Cover & leave soup to simmer for about 10 minutes until pasta is done.

7. Sprinkle each bowl with some permesan cheese then serve warm.

GRANDMA'S CHICKEN 'N' DUMPLING SOUP

Time: 2 hours
Amount: 12 servings

INGREDIENTS

- Fryer/broiler chicken (4 lbs/1.9kg)
- Cold water (2 1/4 quarts)
- Peppercorns (6)
- Condensed chicken soup cream (1 can)
- Condensed mushroom soup cream (1 can)
- Chopped carrots (1 1/2 cups)
- Frozen or fresh Peas-1 cup
- Bay leaf (1)
- Whole cloves (3)
- Onion-chopped (1/4 cup)
- Salt (1 1/2 tsp)
- Pepper (1/4 tsp)

For dumplings:

- 2 cups All-purpose flour
- Pepper (1/4 tsp)
- Egg-1, large
- Salt (1 tsp)
- Butter (2 tbsp, melted)
- Whole milk (3/4 to 1 cup)
- Baking powder (4 tsp)
- Fresh parsley (snipped)- optional

HOW TO COOK

1. Place chicken, bouillon, peppercorns, cloves and water in a pot and cover.

2. Turn on the heat and bring chicken to boil. Skim foam from boiling liquid then turn down heat. Cover and leave to simmer for about 45 minutes to tenderize chicken. Strain broth and return to stockpot

3. Remove the chicken an set aside on a bowl to cool. De-bone the meat and discard bones and skin then cut chicken into chunks. Leave broth to cool and skim off the fat.

4. Add chicken into soup maker along with the broth, seasonings and vegetables then cook for 28 minutes. Remove bay lead and discard it.

5. To prepare dumplings, mix the dry ingredients in a bowl then stir in egg. Add butter and sufficient milk to prepare a moist stiff batter. Drop prepared dumplings into soup in teaspoonfuls. Leave the pot covered for 20 to 25 minutes. Sprinkle some parsley (if desired) and serve.

GRANDMA'S CHICKEN 'N' DUMPLING SOUP

FRESH CORN & POTATO CHOWDER

Time: 40 minutes

Amount: 6 servings

INGREDIENTS

- Onion-chopped (1, medium)
- Butter (1 tbsp)
- Red potatoes (1 pound or 0.45kg)-cubed
- Corn (frozen or fresh)-1 1/2 cups
- Half-n-half cream (1 1/2 cups)-divided
- Chicken broth (reduced-sodium)-3 cups
- Green onions (2, thinly sliced)
- All-purpose flour (3 tsp)
- Salt (1/2 tsp)
- Fresh ground pepper (1/4 tsp)
- Fresh parsley-minced (1 tsp)

HOW TO COOK

1. In a large sauce pan on medium to high heat, cook onion inside butter for about 3 minutes. Be sure to stir as you do to prevent onions from getting stuck on the base of the pan.

2. Add the sauted onion, corn, broth, potatoes, 1 cup cream, green onions, pepper and salt into a soup maker. Cook in the soup maker for 25 or 30 minutes depending on your appliance.

3. Mix flour and remaining cream in a bowl thoroughly until it is very smooth. Stir flour mixture into soup and turn up the heat until it boils.

4. Stir constantly as you cook or until slightly thickened.

5. Add minced parsley and serve hot or warm.

SOUPS WITH MEAT RECIPES

VEGETABLE BEEF SOUP

Time: 45 minutes

Amount: 10 to 12 servings

INGREDIENTS

- Olive oil (1 tbsp)
- Beef stew meat (0.45kg/1 lb) cut to 1inch cubes
- Garlic-minced (3 cloves)
- Carrot-diced (3/4 cup)
- Yukon gold potatoes or russet (3-4)-cubed & peeled
- Diced tomatoes (1 can, 28 oz/793g) with juice
- Worcestershire sauce (1 tbsp)
- Beef stock (4 cups)
- Bay leaves (2)
- Water(1 cup)
- Italian seasoning (1 tbsp)
- Pepper & salt
- Parmesan cheese
- Red pepper flakes(crushed)

HOW TO COOK

1. Heat oil in a sauce pan or large pot

2. Add steaks in batches. Do not crowd the pot.

3. Cook each steak for about 3 minutes on both side until slightly browned.

4 Add onion, garlic, celery, potatoes and carrots. Leave to saute for 4 minutes, stir occasionally. .

5 Add remaining ingredients and transfer into a soup maker. Process soup on chunky or smooth setting as preferred.

6 Season with pepper and salt then serve garnished with some fresh parsley, flakes of red pepper (crushed) and cheese.

STEAK SOUP

Time: 2 hr 20 mins
Amount: 8 servings

INGREDIENTS

- Butter (2 tbsp)
- Vegetable oil (2 tbsp)
- Beef round steak (boneless, cubed)- 0.7kg or 1 1/2 lbs
- Chopped onion (1/2-1 cup)
- Paprika (1 tbsp)
- paprika (1 tbsp)
- All purpose flour-3tbsp
- Black pepper (1/4 tsp)
- Salt (1 tsp)
- Beef broth (4 cups)
- Fresh parsley (4 sprigs, chopped)
- Bay leaf (1)
- Tomato paste (1, 6ounce can)
- Water (2 cups)
- Chopped celery leaves (2 tbsp)
- Marjoram (dried)-1/2 tsp
- Yukon gold potatoes- peeled & diced (1 1/2 cups)
- Carrots-sliced (1 1/2 cups)
- Chopped celery (1 1/2 cups)
- Whole kernel corn (1, 15.25 oz/432g can)-drained

HOW TO COOK

1. Melt oil and butter over medium heat in a large skillet until foam disappears from butter. Stir in the onions and add stead cubes. Cook for about 10 minutes, stirring until the meat & onion are browned

2. While beef cooks, combine flour, pepper, salt and paprika in a bowl. Sprinkle flour mixture over browned meat. Mix well to coat the meat completely.

3. Pour beef the beef broth into soup pot. Add water and stir in celery leaves, parsley, marjoram, and bay leaf. Stir in beef mixture and leave to boil.

4. Turn the heat down to medium low. Leave pot covered to simmer for 45 minutes to tenderize meat. Stir occasionally. Transfer to a soup maker.

5. Add potatoes, celery, carrots, tomato paste, & corn and cook in soup maker until the a thickened soup is formed and vegetable are tenderized.

6. Remove and discard bay leaf.

7. Serve soup hot.

Hearty Beef Soup

Time: 2 hours 20 minutes

Amount: 2 servings

INGREDIENTS

- Beef chuck roast-trimmed & cubed (2 lbs/0.9kg)
- Flour (1/4 cup)
- Paprika (1 tsp)
- Coarsely ground black pepper (1 tsp)
- Unsalted butter (2 tbsp)
- Kosher salt (2tsp)
- Olive oil (2 tsp, extra-virgin)
- Shallot(1, diced)
- Garlic (3 cloves, minced)
- Beef stock (4 cups)
- Worcestershire sauce (2 teaspoons)
- Cabernet Sauvignon (1 cup)
- Italian seasoning
- Red potatoes, chopped (4 cups)
- Baby carrots-chopped into bite-sized pieces (3 cups)
- Fresh parsley (optional garnish)

HOW TO COOK

1. Trim hard fat and silver skin from beef

2. Cut the beef into cubes.

3. In a ziploc bag, mix flour flour, pepper, paprika and salt (1 tsp). Shake the bag vigorously to combine ingredients. Add beef to this mixture then shake well until beef is well coated.

HEARTY BEEF SOUP

4. In a heavy bottomed pot, or large dutch oven, warm olive oil and butter and leave to melt.

5. Remove beef from flour mix then shake gently to get rid of any loose flour on it.

6. Place coated beef in the oil piece by piece (cook in two batches) and cook for about 5 minutes on each sides until browned.

7. Remove meat pieces when browned and place in an upside down pot lid. Repeat this for each of the meat pieces.

8. Prepare garlic and shallot by mincing and dicing respectively.

9. Transfer browned beef, minced garlic and diced shallot to a soup maker.

10. Add the beef stock, Italian seasoning and Worcestershire. Stir to combine. Prepare carrots and potatoes. Add these to the other ingredients in the soupmaker.

11. Cover and cook again for 25 minutes until softened. Taste soup. Add more seasoning if required.

12. To be served garnished with fresh parsley if desired.

CHICKEN EASY CROCK POT MEATBALL SOUP

Time: 10 hours 5 minutes
Amount: 6-servings

INGREDIENTS

- Potato (1, medium)
- Onion (1, small)
- Frozen meatballs (1 lb/0.45kg)-italian seasoned
- Ground black pepper (1/4 tsp)
- Beef stock (3 cups)
- Garlic powder (1/2 tsp)
- Mixed vegetables (frozen, 1-16oz/450gpacl)
- Black pepper (1/4 tsp)

HOW TO COOK

1. Prepare ingredients; peel potatoes and dice, peel onion and chop finely

2. Mix frozen meatballs, potatoes, chopped onion, garlic powder, beef stock and tomatoes in a slow cooker. Cover and cook for about 6 to 8 hours until ingredients are all tender.

3. Transfer to a soup maker. Add frozen vegetables to the mix and stir.

4. Cover soup maker and cook on smooth setting for about 30 minutes. Serve soup when ready.

Time: 50 minutes

Amount: 4 portions

INGREDIENTS

- Meat and bones form one chicken (4 lbs/1.8kg)
- Carrots (2, medium) sliced into rounds-about 1/4 inch thick
- Chicken broth (4 cups, low-sodium broth preferably)
- Celery stalks-sliced-1/4 inch thick
- Chopped Onion (1 medium,)
- Bay leaf
- White rice (1/2 cup)
- Parsley (chopped-2 tbsp)
- Kosher salt

HOW TO COOK

1. Put carcass and bones form leftover chicken in a large pot

2. Cover with broth. Pour water into the pot (about 4 cups). cover and bring to boil on medium to high heat then turn the heat down.

3. Leave to simmer like this for about 20 minutes skimming faom or fat from the broth with a laddle as you cook.

4. Using a slotted spoon or thongs, remove carcass and bones. Leave broth aside for a while until it cools.

SIMPLE CHICKEN SOUP

SIMPLE CHICKEN SOUP

5. Pour broth into a soup maker. Add celery, carrots, onion and bay leaf. Cook for about 10 minutes and turn off soup maker when the vegetables are half-cooked.

6. Stir in rice and turn soup maker on again for about 12 minutes.

7. Pick off meat from carcass and shred into small bite-sized pieces

8. Add the shredded meat to the broth when rice is ready. Stir in parsley & add 1/2 tsp of salt or more to season.

9. Serve hot.

THE ULTIMATE CHICKEN NOODLE SOUP

Time: 1 hour

Amount: 6 portions

INGREDIENTS

- Pepper (1 1/4 tsp) divided
- Chicken thighs (with the bones) -1.3 kg or 2 1/2 lbs
- Salt (1/2 tsp)
- Canola oil (1 tbsp)
- Onion (1-large, chopped)
- Garlic clove (1, minced)
- Chicken broth (10 cups)
- Celery ribs (4, chopped)
- Carrots (4, medium)
- Bay leaves (2)
- Minced fresh thyme (1 tsp) (or dried (1/4 tsp)
- Kluski or any egg noodles (3 cups)
- Chopped fresh parsley (1 tbsp)
- Lemon juice (1 tbsp)

HOW TO COOK

1. Pat chicken dry with paper towels then sprinkle with salt and pepper

2. Heat the canola oil in a sauce pan over medium to high heat. Add chicken to oil in batches with the skin side down.

3. Cook each chicken for about 4 minutes on each side until it turns a dark golden brown color. Remove from pan and repeat for all the chicken pieces.

THE ULTIMATE CHICKEN NOODLE SOUP

4. Remove & discard skin and drippings (reserve 2 tbsp of drippings)

5. Transfer reserved dripping into a soup maker, add onion, garlic and broth. Stir repeatedly then turn on soup maker to cook and blend ingredients are tenderized.

6. Transfer soup from the soup maker to a pot.

7. To the soup, add the noddle, cover and leave for 20 to 22 minutes until noodles tenderize.

8. When the chicken earlier set aside cools, remove bones from the meat and discard. Shred meat into smaller bite-size pieces. Add chicken to the soup in the pot.

9. Add the parsely and lemon juice and season with salt and remaining pepper.

10. Remove and discard bay leave.

Time: 35 minutes

Amount: serves 4

INGREDIENTS

- Chopped onion (1 cup)
- Chopped green bell pepper (2/3 cup)
- Jalapeno pepper (1, seeded & minced)
- Minced garlic (1 tbsp)
- Pork tenderloin-trimmed and cut into small bite-size bits (1 lb/ 0.45kg)
- Low sodium chicken broth (2 cups, fat free)
- Chilli powder (2 tsp)
- Ground cumin (1 tsp)
- Pink beans (1 15oz can)- rinsed & drained
- Salt (1/2 tsp)
- Diced tomatoes (1, 15oz can)- undrained
- Diced avocado (1 cup)
- Fresh cilantro (2 tbsp, chopped)
- Black pepper (1tsp)

SOUTHWESTERN PORK SOUP

HOW TO COOK

1. In a sauce pan or stock pot coated with cooking spray add bell pepper, onion, garlic and jalapeno to saute for 3 minutes

2. Add int the pork and allow to cook for 3 more minutes.

3. Put sauted ingredients into a soup maker. Add broth, chilli powder, ground cumin, salt, black pepper, diced tomatoes and pink beans then cook.

4. Remove from heat. Stir in cilantro and serve with some avocados

VEGETABLE PORK SOUP

Time: 40 minutes

Amount: 4 portions

INGREDIENTS

- Pork loin chop (1, boneless) cut into cubes.
- Smoked kielbasa (1/4 lb/0.1kg) or polish sausage
- ChoppedOnion (1/4 cup)
- Chopped celery rib (1)
- Minced garlic clove (1)
- Chopped carrot (1, small)
- Paprika (1/4 teaspoon)
- Chopped tart apple (1, small)
- Red potato (1, small)
- Honey (1 teaspoon)
- Chinese five-spice powder (1/4 teaspoon)

HOW TO COOK

1. Cook pork, sausage, onion, celery and carrots in butter in a large saucepan on medium-high heat. Cook for about 5 minutes to tenderize vegetables and until the pork is no longer pink.

2. Transfer pork and the tenderized vegetables to a soup maker. Add garlic and paprika and stir in the broth, apple, potato and five-spice powder.

3. Cook in soup maker to tenderize the pork. You can cook on either smooth or chunky setting as preferred.

4. Stir in the honey and return to a pot. Cook for an additional 2 minutes to warm up the soup.

5. Serve hot.

SOUP MAKER TURKEY & HAM CREAM SOUP

Time: 10 minutes

Amount: 2 servings

INGREDIENTS

- Cooked turkey breast (200g/7oz)
- Soft cheese (200g/7oz)
- Cooked ham (100g/3.5oz)
- Cheddar cheese (100g/3.5oz)
- Tarragon (3 tbsp)
- Chives (1 tbsp)
- Chicken stock (250ml)
- Pepper
- Salt
- Croutons (optional)

HOW TO COOK

1. Place turkey breast and ham in soup maker. Add the chicken stock and turn on the soup maker.

2. Cook on chunky setting for 25 to 28 minutes.

3. Stop the soup maker and open.

4. Reduce stock by half then add the remaining ingredients. Turn on the soup maker again to blend ingredients.

5. Can be served with croutons.

BOLOGNESE BEEF SOUP

Time: 20 minutes

Amount: serves 2 to 4 people

INGREDIENTS

- Cooked lean beef mince (200g/7oz)
- Olive oil (1tbsp)
- 3 garlic cloves (crushed)
- Mixed herbs (2 tsp)
- Tinned tomatoes (400g/14ozcan)
- Beef stock (750g/26.5oz)

HOW TO COOK

1. Brown minced beef in oil. Remove from heat and drain off excess fat.

2. Saute onion in olive oil as well.

3. Add crushed garlic, mixed herbs and chopped tomatoes to soup maker. Add the beef stock and the cooked minced along with sauted onion.

4. Stir to combine well. Cover the soup maker and cook content on smooth setting for about 30 minutes.

SOUP WITH FISH RECIPES

SOUP WITH FISH RECIPES

FISH AND VEGETABLE SOUP

Time: 35 minutes

Amount: 4 servings

INGREDIENTS

- Margarine/butter (1 tsp)
- Chopped onion (1/4 cup)
- Finely chopped garlic clove (1)
- Progresso™ chicken broth (3 1/2 Cups)
- Salt (1/2 tsp)
- Carrots (1 cup, sliced)
- Frozen corn (1/2 cup)
- Frozen Greenbeans (1 cup)
- Oregano leaves (1/4 teaspoons)
- Pepper (1/8 tsp)
- Basil leaves (1/2 tsp)
- White fish fillets (0.45kg or 1lb) (cubed, about 1 inch each)

HOW TO MAKE

1. In a saucepan or dutch oven, melt butter on medium heat.

2. Add garlic and onions to melted butter and saute for about 3 minutes until they are just beginning to turn brown.

3. Add in sauted ingredients and all the remaining ingredient and the fish into a soup maker cover soup maker and cook on smooth or chunky setting.

4. Serve soup when ready.

SICILIAN FISH SOUP

Time: 1 hour

Amount: 6 servings

INGREDIENTS

- Red onion (1)
- Celery (2 sticks)
- Fennel (1/2 small bulb)
- Garlic (2 cloves)
- Red chilli (1, de-seeded)
- Olive oil (2 or 3 tbsp, plus more for drizzling)
- White wine (1 glass)
- Plum tomatoes (800g, chopped) or passata
- Butternut squash (1/2) peeled and grated
- Organic fish stock (500ml)
- Salmon fillet (200g/7oz)
- Halibut fillet (300g/10.5oz)
- Raw prawns (12, peeled) or langoustine tails
- 1/2 lemon
- Fresh parsley (1 large, chopped)

HOW TO COOK

1. Chop onions, fennel, celery, garlic and chilli.

2. In a large saucepan, heat oil and add in the finely chopped fennel, onions, celery, chilli and garlic. Cook gently until softened. Transfer sweated ingredients into a soup maker.

3. Add wine, passata or tomatoes, squash and stock then cook in the soup maker for 30 minutes.

SICILIAN FISH SOUP

4. Season and break the tomatoes gently with a spoon.

5. Chop fish fillets roughly and pour it into the soup. Add prawns and cook for 10 additional minutes until it is just cooked..

6. Taste the soup then add more salt, pepper and a squeeze of lemon juice if required.

7. Grate butternut squash into the soup

8. Serve drizzled with oil with chopped parsley as garnish.

Time: 35 minutes

Amount: 5 servings

INGREDIENTS

- Butter (3 tbsp)
- Minced garlic cloves (2)
- Finely chopped onion (1, small)
- Carrots (2, small) halved and cut into slices about 1.5 inch/0.5cm thick
- White wine (1/2 cup)-optional
- Milk (3 cups)
- Flour (1/4 cup)
- Fish stock, chicken stock or clam juice (2 cups)
- Potato (2 cups, cubed)
- Frozen or canned corn (1 cup, with the fluid drained)
- Salt (1/2 tsp)
- Black pepper (finely ground)
- White fish fillets (1.2 lb 0.6g)
- Frozen peas (1 cup)

HOW TO COOK

1. Cook garlic & onion in butter in a saucepan over medium heat until translucent (for about 5 minutes.

2. Add carrots then turn the heat up to high. Add in the wine, stir then leave to simmer until the wine is mostly evaporated

3. Transfer to a soup maker and add flour then stir to form a sludge

4. Slowly pour in the broth while still stirring to dissolve the paste

FISH CHOWDER SOUP

FISH CHOWDER SOUP

5 Stir in the milk then add potato, corn, pepper and salt. Turn on the soup maker and cook soup on smooth or chunky setting.

6 Add fish & peas then leave soup for about 3 minutes to simmer until the fish is just cooked right.

7 Taste & add some more seasoning if required.

8 You can add water or milk if soup is too thick.

9 Serve garnished with crusty bread and green onions on the side for dunking.

Time: 30 minutes

Amount:serves 4

INGREDIENTS

- Onions (1, diced)
- Minced garlic (4 cloves)
- Celery (2 stalks, diced)
- Olive oil (2 tbsp)
- Green pepper (1, cubed)
- Lemon juice (extracted from 1 medium lemon)
- Dry white wine (1/2 cup)
- Salt (1/2 tsp)
- Italian seasoning (2 tsp)
- Diced tomatoes (2-14.5oz/411g can)- undrained
- Black pepper (1/2 tsp)
- Chicken or fish stock (2 cups)
- Tomato paste (2 tbsp)
- Alaska cod or any whitefish (16oz/453g)
- Chopped fresh basil (3 tbsp)

HOW TO COOK

| 1 | Heat oil in a sauce pan or pot |

| 2 | Cook onions in pot for 5 to 8 minutes until fragrant. Be sure to stir as it cooks. |

| 3 | Transfer sauted onion to a soup maker. Stir in celery, bell pepper and garlic |

| 4 | Add lemon juice, wine, Italian seasoning, salt & pepper. |

EASY ITALIAN FISH SOUP

EASY ITALIAN FISH SOUP

5. Stir in tomato chunks, chicken or fish stock & the tomato paste. Cover soup maker and cook on chunky soup setting.

6. Cut fish into smaller bits and stir into soup. Bring to boil slightly then leave for about 5 minutes until fish is tender.

7. Remove from heat, add basil, stir and serve

UMBRIAN FISH SOUP

Time: 45 minutes

Amount: serves 6

INGREDIENTS

- Chopped onion (1/2 cup)
- Fresh water fish fillets (2lbs/0/9kg)-cut into small pieces
- Chopped celery (1/2 cup)
- Choppedflat-leaf parsley (1/4 cup)
- 4 garlic cloves (finely chopped)
- White wine (1 cup)
- Olive oil (1/2 cup)
- Crushed can tomatoes (1, 28oz/793g can)
- Water (2 cups)

For toasts

- 1baguette
- Olive oil (2 tbsp)
- Garlic clove (1)
- Flat-leaf parsley for garnishing

HOW TO COOK

1. Pat the fish dry and sprinkle with some salt (about 1/2 tsp)
2. Cook onion, garlic and celery in oil over medium heat. Add 1/2 tsp salt.
3. Stir as you cook for about 5 to 8 minutes until ingredients are softened.
4. Add parsley and cook for an additional minute,

UMBRIAN FISH SOUP

5. Pour sauted ingredients into a soup maker, add wine, tomatoes, water and about 1 tsp salt then add in the fish turn the soup maker on and run on chunky or smooth.

6. To prepare toasts preheat broiler, slice baguette & toast about 3- inches from heat. Turn regularly to ensure that all sides are evenly cooked. Cook for about 4 minutes or until all sides turn a golden color. to ensure even cooking for about 4 minutes or until golden on all sides.

7. Half the garlic cloves and rub them on the toast. Brush toasts with oil and serve with soup.

SOPA DE PESCADO

Time: 25 minutes

Amount: 4 servings

INGREDIENTS

- Sea bass fillet (or any tropical fish)-1.5 lbs/0.7kg
- Olive oil (2 tbsp)
- Juice (from 1 lime)
- Sliced garlic cloves (2)
- Diced carrot (1, large)
- Auyama (kaboach squash or West Indian pumpkin) diced and divided
- Water (2 quarts/2 lt)
- Cilantro (2 sprigs)
- Salt (1.5 tsp)

HOW TO MAKE

1. Mix half the fish, lime juice, oil, pumpkin and garlic in soup maker. Add some water & cook for about 25 to 28 minutes.

2. Turn off the soup maker and sieve to remove the solid.

3. Pour broth back into the soup maker. Add carrot, cilantro, potato and the remaining auyama pumpkin. Cook covered on chunky soup setting.

4. Add the remaining fish to the soup then cook for about 15 minutes until have of the liquid you started with it gone. You may add more water if the soup is too thick.

5. Add some salt to season and serve hot.

FISH SOUP FOR WINTER DINNERS

Time: 1 hour

Amount: 4 servings

INGREDIENTS

- Olive oil (2 tbsp, more for serving)
- Deboned fish (2 lbs, 0.9kg)
- Onion (1, medium)
- Garlic cloves (3, large)
- Tomato (1, large)
- Celery (2 stalks)
- Carrot (1 large)
- Saffron (a pinch)
- Bell pepper (1/2, red)
- Tender leek (1 fresh)
- Dried of fresh thyme (1 pinch/1 sprig)
- Bay leaves (2)
- Salt (2tsp)
- Black pepper (1/4 tsp)
- Chopped cilantro or parsley (1 handful)

HOW TO COOK

1. Peel & chop your vegetables into chunks.

2. Saute all the vegetables except the bell peppers in olive oil

3. Add salt, pepper, bay leaves and thyme.

4. Cover the pan & leave ingredients to steam for 10 minutes. Transfer sweated ingredients into a soup maker.

5. Add water until ingredients are covered. Add saffron and vegetable stock then add fishes, if using more than one kind of fish, add the firmer pieces first.

6. Turn on soup maker and cook for about 20 minutes. Add delicate fish pieces & the red pepper then cook for an additional 10 minutes.

7. Add chopped cilantro or parsley and pulse soup maker to mix.

8. Add a splash of oil to each serving boil then serve soup with plenty of hot garlic bread.

MEDITERRANEAN FISH SOUP

Time: 30 minutes

Amount: 6 servings

INGREDIENTS

- Olive oil (2 tbsp)
- Onion (1 large, chopped)
- Dry white wine (1/4 cup)
- Organic vegetable or chicken (4 cups)
- Diced tomatoes (1 14.5oz/411g can)
- Mussel (24), scrubbed, beards removed
- White fish fillets (1 lb/0.45kg)- you can use cod, halibut or haddock
- Frozen or fresh large shrimps (1/2 lb/0.27kg) peeled and deveined
- Fresh basil leaves, shredded (2 tbsp)

HOW TO COOK

1. In a 6-quart suacepot heat oil and cook onions until tenderized
2. Add the dry white wine & cook for 1 minute then transfer to a soup maker
3. Stir in the broth and the tomatoes.
4. Also add in the fish, shrimp and mussels. Cover and cook in soup maker until the mussels open and the fish flakes when tested with fork
5. Sieve and discard any mussels that are not open. Taste and add seasoning as desired.
6. Serve hot. You can garnish with basil if desired.

SPICY FISH SOUP

Time: 40 minutes

Amount: 4 servings

INGREDIENTS

- onion (1/2, chopped)
- Minced garlic (1 clove)
- Chilli powder (1 tbsp)
- Canned green chilli pepper (1-4oz/113g can)- chopped
- Ground cumin (1 tsp)
- Chicken broth (1.5 cups)
- Canned tomatoes (diced and peeled) (1.5 cup)
- Cod fillets (1/2 lb/0.27kg)
- Green bell pepper (chopped, 1/2 cup)
- Shrimp (1/2 cup)
- Nonfat yogurt (1/2 lb/ 0.27kg)
- Cod fillets (1/2 lb/0.27kg)

HOW TO COOK

1. Prepare a saucepan by spraying it with some cooking spray. Place over medium-high heat and add onions to saute for about 4 minutes

2. Add garlic and chilli powder and saute for an additional minute

3. Add chicken broth, cumin and chilli peppers. Stir and bring to boil.

4. Transfer soup to soup maker, add tomatoes, shrimp, cod & green bell pepper. Cook in soup maker on smooth setting for about 25 minutes

5. Return soup back to a pot. Cover and leave to simmer for 5 minutes.

6. Gradually add the yogurt until it is heated through.

QUICK EASY FISH STEW

Time: 20 minutes

Amount: 4 servings

INGREDIENTS

- Extra virgin olive oil (6 tbsp)
- Onion (1 medium, chopped)
- Garlic cloves (3, large- minced)
- Freshtomatoes - (chopped, 1 1/2 cups)
- Fresh parsley (2/3 cup)
- Tomato paste (2 tsp)
- Clam juice (8oz) or shellfish stock
- Dry white wine (1/2 cup)
- Fish fillets (use any white fish) (1.5lb or 0.7kg)
- Dry oregano (a pinch)
- Fresh ground pepper
- salt (to taste)
- Dry thyme (a pinch)
- Tabasco sauce (1/8 tsp)

HOW TO COOK

1. In a large thick bottomed pot placed heat olive oil and saute onions for about 4 minutes.

2. Add in garlic then cook for an additional minute. Add parsley and cook for 2 more minutes while stirring.

3 Add sauted onions and garlic, tomatoes and tomato paste, clam juice or shell fish stock and white wine into a soup maker and cook for about 25 minutes.

4 Add seasoning, salt & pepper to taste.

5 Serve in bowls. Can be served with crusty bread for dipping.

CREAM SOUP RECIPES

CREAM SOUP RECIPES

CREAMY CHICKEN AND MUSHROOM SOUP

Time: 35 minutes

Amount: 4 servings

INGREDIENTS

- Olive oil (1 tbsp)
- Skinless chicken thighs (8 oz)-skinless & boneless
- Unsalted butter (2 tbsp)
- Kosher salt
- Garlic cloves (3) minced
- Freshly ground black pepper
- Onion (1, diced)
- Cremini Mushrooms (8 oz/) thinly sliced
- Carrot (3 peeled & diced)
- Celery (2 stalks (diced)
- Thyme (1/2 tsp, dried)
- All purpose flour (1/4 cup)
- Bay leaf (1)
- Half-n-half (1/2 cup)
- Fresh parsley leaves (2 tbsp)
- Rosemary (1 sprig)

HOW TO MAKE

1. Pour olive oil into a saucepan or pot over medium heat

2. Add pepper & salt to chicken thighs to season and cook in olive oil for about 3 minutes on both sides until golden. Remove and set aside

3. Melt butter in stockpot. Add mushrooms, garlic, celery and garlic. Cook for about 4 minutes. Stir occasionally. Add thyme and cook for 1 more minute.

4 Whisk in flour for about 1 minute until browned lightly. Transfer to a soup maker.

5 Add chicken stock, chicken thighs and bay leave. Cook in soup maker until soup is slightly thick.

6 Stir in half-n-half seasoning, salt & pepper to season. Add more half and half to soup then pulse in soup maker to mix.

7 To be served immediately garnished with rosemary and parsley if desired.

QUICK CREAM OF MUSHROOM SOUP

Time: 30 minutes

Amount: 6 servings

INGREDIENTS

- Butter (2 tbsp)
- Chopped onion (1/4 cup)
- Fresh mushrooms (1/2 lb or 0.27 kg)
- All purpose flour (6 tsp)
- Salt (1/2 tsp)
- Pepper (1/8 tsp)
- Chicken broth (2, 14.5oz/411gcans)
- Half-and-half (1 cup)

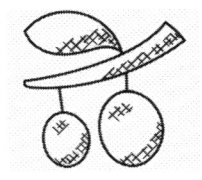

HOW TO COOK

1. In a large saucepan, heat butter over medium-high heat. Add onions & mushroom then saute for some minutes until tender.

2. mushrooms until tender

3. Mix flour, pepper, salt and 1 can chicken broth until smooth. Stir this into mushroom mixture in a soup maker then stir in the remaining broth and cook on smooth until thickened.

4. Turn off the soup maker and stir in cream. Pulse to mix until consistency and thickness is as desired.

HOMEMADE CREAMY VEGETABLE SOUP

Time: 30 minutes

Amount: serves 5

INGREDIENTS

- Olive oil (1 tsp)
- Butter (2tbsp)
- Onions (1/2 cup)
- Celery (1/2 cup, chopped)
- Minced garlic (1 tbsp)
- Broccoli florets (1 cup)
- Dried thyme (1 tsp)
- Carrots (1 cup, chopped)
- Green beans(1 cup, chopped)
- Sliced mushrooms (1 cup)
- Corn kernels (1 cup)
- Oregano (1tsp, dried)
- All purpose flour (3 tbsp)
- Whole milk (4 cups)
- Pepper & salt

HOW TO COOK

1. Saute onions, celery and carrots in olive oil & butter for a few minutes to soften.

2. Add beans, mushrooms, garlic, corn and broccoli and saute for 3 additional minutes.

3. Add thyme, dried oregano, flour, whole milk, pepper and salt then cook in soup maker until soup thickens to desired consistency.

4. Add a little more milk or broth to thin out if too thick. Serve hot

CREAMY CHICKEN SOUP

Time: 30 minutes

Amount: 4 servings

INGREDIENTS

- Olive oil (1 tsp)
- Chicken thighs (1 lb/0.45kg) skinless
- White wine (1/2 cup)
- Butter (5 tsp, divided)
- Onion (1, minced)
- Celery stalks (4, diced)
- Garlic cloves (3, minced)
- Flour (6 tbsp)
- Milk (1.5 cups)
- Heavy cream (1 cup)
- Carrots (2, large) peeled and diced
- Chicken broth (4 cups)
- Salt

HOW TO COOK

1. Cook the chicken thighs in olive oil inside a saucepan place over medium heat.

2. Remove chicken from heat and leave aside on a plate to cool.

3. Deglaze pan with white wine & scrape the base of the pan to remove chicken bit that are stuck on it. Transfer the bits of chicken along with the white wine into a cup.

4. Add 1 tsp of butter to an heavy bottomed pot and turn the heat up to high. Add all sauted ingredients (celery, onions and carrots) into the pot and cook for about 9 minutes until slightly browned.

5. Shred chicken meat while vegetables are cooking. Remove vegetables form heat and set them on the plate with the chicken.

6. In a soup maker, add butter, garlic, flour, heavy cream, milk as well as the earlier set aside chicken and vegetables. Cook for 25 minutes on smooth or chunky setting as desired.

7. Add pepper & salt to season.

8. Can be served with rosemary crackers or crusty bread.

BEST HOMEMADE CREAM OF CELERY SOUP

Time: 30 minutes

Amount: 4 servings

INGREDIENTS

- Butter (1/4 cup)
- Yellow onion (1 small, chopped)
- Finely chopped celery (2 cups)- organic recommended
- Garlic clove (1 large, minced)
- Unbleached flour (1/3 cup)
- Chicken broth (1.5 cups)
- Whole milk (1 1/2 cups)
- Freshly ground pepper (1/8 tsp)
- Salt (1 tsp)
- Sugar (1/2 tsp)

HOW TO COOK

1. Melt butter in a saucepan over medium to high heat. Add garlic, onions and celery and cook until softened (about 7 minutes)

2. Transfer to soup maker and add flour, milk and chicken broth and remaining ingredients then turn on the soup maker.

3. Season with salt (to taste) you can keep soup in the refrigerator for as much as 4 days.

QUICK AND EASY CREAMY VEGETABLE SOUP

Time: 35 minutes

Amount: 4 servings

INGREDIENTS

- Onion (1 large)
- Carrots (1 lb/0.45kg)
- Celery (4 sticks)
- Olive oil (1 tbsp)
- Red pepper flakes (crushed, 1/4 tsp)
- Thin-skinned potatoes (1 lb/0.45kg)
- Garlic cloves (3, peeled & halved)
- Chicken or vegetable stock (3 cups)
- Bay leaves
- Fresh thyme (3 sprigs)
- Coconut milk (1/4 cup) or coconut cream
- Salt

HOW TO MAKE

1. Chop onions, celery and carrots into chunks.

2. Chop potatoes into the same size but set aside separately

3. Toss vegetables into heated oil in a large pot. Add salt & crushed red pepper flakes. Cook like this for about 5 - 10 minutes until vegetables are soft. Be sure to stir occasionally as you cook.

4. Stir in garlic, thyme, potatoes and bay leaves. Cook for about 4 minutes

5. Transfer vegetables and potatoes to soup maker, add stock and cook for about 25 minutes on chunky setting (or smooth if desired).

CREAM OF TOMATO SOUP RECIPE

Time: 45 minutes

Amount: 6 servings

INGREDIENTS

- Onion (1 choppedO
- Butter (25g/0.8oz)
- Paprika (1 tsp)
- Garlic (1 clove, crushed)
- Tomato puree (1 tbsp)
- Sugar (2 tsp)
- Bay leaf (1)
- Vegetable stock (600ml)
- Double cream (142ml)
- Basil leaves (optional)

HOW TO COOK

1. Cook onions in the butter until softened (for about 10 minutes). Add paprika and garlic then cook for about 2 more minutes

2. Add tomato puree. Cook for 2 more minutes then add sugar, bay leaf, vegetable to chicken stock and cook in a soup maker for about 25 minutes. You can cook in batches if required.

3. Sieve to remove any skin or seeds and return the liquid to rinsed out pan.

4. Stir in some of the double cream (2/3) and reheat the soup gently.

5. You can add a swirl of more cream and some basil leaves to garnish and serve immediately.

Time: 15 minutes

Amount: 8 servings

INGREDIENTS

- Butter (1/2 cup)
- All purpose flour (6 tsp)
- Milk (2 cups)
- Ground black pepper
- Chicken bouillon (2 cubes)

HOW TO COOK

1. In a saucepan, melt butter and add flour to make a paste. To this, add bouillon cubes and milk.

2. Cook in soup maker until thickened.

3. Add pepper as desired. Add other other soup ingredients and more milk if desired.

4. You may add steamed broccoli, American cheese, chives and bacon pieces to this base.

CREAM SOUP BASE

CREAMY ROASTED CAULIFLOWER SOUP

Time: 1 hour

Amount: serves 4

INGREDIENTS

- Fine sea salt
- Extra-virgin olive oil (4 bsp, divided)
- Cauliflower (1 large head cut into bite-sized florets)
- Chopped onion (1 medium, red)
- Vegetable broth (4 cups)
- Minced or pressed garlic (2 cloves)
- Unsalted butter (2 tbsp)
- Lemon juice(fresh, 1 tbsp or more)
- Ground nutmeg (1/4 tsp)

Garnish:

- Finely chopped parsley, chives or green onion

HOW TO COOK

1. Preheat the oven to 425 °F/200°C. Prepare your baking sheet. Line sheet with parchment paper.

2. Toss cauliflower along with 2 tbsp olive oil on baking sheet. Ensure that the cauliflower is evenly coated with oil. Arrange cauliflower on baking sheet in a single layer then sprinkle with salt.

3. Bake for about 25 to 35 minutes until cauliflower is softened and caramelized on the edges. Flip half-way through baking

4. Warm the rest of the olive oil in a sauce pan over medium heat. Add onion and salt to this and saute for 7 minutes or less stirring occasionally stirring occasionally as you do until the onion softens

5. Add garlic & cook for 30 seconds more until fragrant then add broth.

6. Reserve 4 roasted cauliflower floret to be used as garnish when soup is ready. Transfer the remaining florets and all the other prepared ingredients into a soup maker.

7. Turn on the soup maker and cook mixture on smooth settings for about 20 to 25 minutes. Add in nutmeg and lemon juice then pulse. Taste and add salt or lemon jiuce if more is needed.

8. Top each bowl with 1 roasted cauliflower and a sprinkle of parsley, chives or green onion.

CLASSICAL SOUPS RECIPE: CREAMY POTATO SOUP

Time: 40 minutes

Amount: 5 servings

INGREDIENTS

- Butter (2 tbsp)
- Onion (1, medium)
- Celery (1 stalk, thinly sliced)
- Potato (3, medium) - peeled & cubed
- Chicken broth (1 3/4 cups)
- Milk (1 1/2 cups)
- Chopped fresh parsley (1 tablespoon)

HOW TO COOK

1. Heat butter over medium heat in a 3-quart saucepan. Add onion & celery then cook until tenderized.

2. Stir potatoes and broth into a soup maker along with tenderized onion & celery. turn the soup maker on and cook covered for about 25 minutes.

3. Add milk to the soup mixture and pulse until well mixed

4. Return soup to stock pot and heat through. Add more seasoning to taste if needed.

5. Serve with parsley as garnish

VEGETARIAN SOUP RECIPES

VEGETARIAN TORTILLA SOUP

Time: 35 minutes

Amount: 4 to 6 servings

INGREDIENTS

- 6 Corn tortillas (6 inches each)
- Kosher salt
- Olive oil
- Onion (1, yellow)
- Bell pepper (1, green)
- Garlic cloves (4, medium)
- Black beans (2 cans, 15oz)
- Extra virgin olive oil (2 tbsp)
- Dried oregano (2 tsp)
- Cumin (1 tsp)
- Crushed tomatoes (1 can, 28oz)
- Frozen or fire-roasted corn (1½ cups)
- Vegetable broth (4 cups)
- Kosher salt
- 4 radishes
- Cilantro (1 handful)
- Lime (1)

HOW TO MAKE

1. Prepare tortillas by brushing them with olive oil lightly on each side. Slice tortillas in half with a pizza cuter then cut them into thin strips.

2. Place strips of tortillas on baking sheets, sprinkle kosher salt & bake in preheated oven.

3. Bake until lightly browned & crispy (for about 12 minutes)

84

4. Peel and dice onion, dice green pepper and peel garlic then mince. Also drain & rinse the beans

5. In a saucepan, heat 2 tbsp of oil. Saute onions in olive oil for 5 minutes until translucent. To this, add some garlic & green pepper and saute for an additional 2 minutes. Stir in the cumin and oregano then cook for 1 more minute.

6. Transfer content to a soup maker. Add in tomatoes, corn, beans, broth, kosher salt and turn soup maker on.

7. Ladle soup into bowls & leave to cool slightly.

8. Garnish with tortilla strips, cilantro leaves, radishes, hot sauce and lime wedges.

VEGETABLE TORTELLINI SOUP

Time: 15 minutes

Amount: 4 servings

INGREDIENTS

- Zucchini (1, cut intochunks about 1/2 inch each)
- Tortellini (1 cup, dried)
- Carrot (1, cut intochunks about 1/2 inch each)
- Onion (1/2 medium, chopped)
- Leek (1, small) only white & greenpart should be cut into smaller bits
- Low-sodium vegetable broth (3 cups)
- Pepper and salt (added to taste)

HOW TO COOK

1. Put all the ingredients into a soup maker. Stir and close lid.
2. Select chunky setting and start the soup maker
3. Open the soup maker and serve soup into bowls when ready.

GREEK EAT YOUR GREENS SLIMMING WORLD SPEED SOUP

Time: 35 minutes

Amount: 2 servings

INGREDIENTS

- Broccoli (100g)
- Courgette (1/2 medium)
- Savoy cabbage (100g)
- Asparagus (4 spears)
- Frozen peas (1 handful)
- Fresh spinach (1 handful)
- Garlic puree (2 tsp)
- Fresh thyme (1 tbsp)
- Vegetable OXO cube
- Parsley (1 tsp)
- Fresh mint (1 tbsp)
- Thyme (1 tbsp)
- Greek yogurt (1 tsp)
- Pepper & salt

HOW TO COOK

1	Clean all fresh Ingredients
2	Chop broccoli into florets and the asparagus into slices about 1cm each. Also, slice up all the other fresh herbs as well as the spinach and cabbage
3	Place all vegetables into the soup maker
4	Add 200ml of water on top

87

GREEK EAT YOUR GREENS SLIMMING WORLD SPEED SOUP

5. Add all seasonings

6. Cover the soup maker and cook for about 25 minutes

7. Add garlic and stir vegetables until well mixed then pulse for some minutes.

8. Can be served with a tsp of yogurt

SOUP MAKER LENTIL SOUP

Time: 34 minutes

Amount:2 servings

INGREDIENTS

- Red lentils (100g/3.5oz)
- Large onion (1/2 medium)
- 2 garlic (2 cloves)
- Carrots (4 large)
- Tomatoes (6 medium)
- Red chai curry (1 tsp)
- Vegetable OXO cube-optional

HOW TO COOK

1. Clean and dice vegetables and season with sea salt
2. Rinse red lentils and place in soup maker along with vegetables
3. Add vegetable stock, seasoning and salt
4. Cover soup maker & cook for 25 to 30 minutes and serve.

PORTUGUESE GREEN BEAN & CARROT SOUP

Time: 30 minutes

Amount: 2 servings

INGREDIENTS

- Beans (400g/14oz thinly diced)
- Carrots (400g/14oz thinly diced)
- Vegetable stock (250 ml)
- Parsley (1 tbsp)
- Pepper and salt

HOW TO COOK

1. Place carrots and green beans in a soup maker
2. Add other ingredients and cover the device
3. Set the soup maker to chunky mode and blend until smooth.

Time: 35 minutes

Amount: 4 servings

INGREDIENTS

- White cabbage (1/3)
- Pepper (1 green)
- Pepper (1 red)
- Carrots (4 large)
- Celery (3 sticks)
- Tomatoes (2 large)
- Water (100ml)
- Pepper and salt (as desired)
- Oregano (1tsp)

HOW TO MAKE

1. Peel carrots, and prepare peppers by washing and de-seeding then chop all into small bits

2. Put all your ingredients into the soup maker. Add water and some seasoning and turn soup maker on.

3. Cook for about 25 minutes then serve.

DECONSTRUCTED SALAD SOUP

HEALTHY GREEN SOUP

Time: 35 minutes

Amount: 4 servings

INGREDIENTS

- Cabbage (1/3 Large)
- Green pepper (1 medium)
- Broccoli (1 medium)
- Thyme (1 tsp)
- Parsley (1 tsp)
- Mustard (1 tsp)
- Water (100 ml)
- Pepper & salt

HOW TO COOK

1. Slice up cabbage, broccoli, and courgette
2. De-seed pepper and dice it
3. Place all vegetables in the soup maker. Add seasoning & water
4. Cover and power on soup maker. Cook for about 25 minutes
5. Turn off unit and serve soup.

Time: 28 minutes

Amount: 4 servings

INGREDIENTS

- Frozen garden peas (1/2 kg/0.3lb)
- Onions (2, peeled)
- Greek yogurt (2 tbsp)
- Fresh mint (1 tsp)
- Mozzarella (50g)
- Water (250ml)
- Garlic puree (1 tsp)
- Parsley (1 tbsp)
- Pepper and salt (as desired)

HOW TO COOK

1	Place peas, seasoning, mozarella and greek yogurt in soup maker
2	Dice onion and add then add water
3	Cook in soup maker for about 25 minutes
4	Check and add some water or yogurt if desired
5	Serve

CREAM OF BROCCOLI SOUP

Time: 30 minutes

Amount: 4 servings

INGREDIENTS

- Courgette (1/5 medium)
- Broccoli (1 medium)
- Oregano (1 tsp)
- Thyme (1 tsp)
- Water (470ml)
- Pepper & salt
- Greek yogurt (2 tbsp)

HOW TO COOK

1. Chop vegetables and pour into soup maker. Cut broccoli into medium sized florets and add as well
2. Add water and seasoning
3. Turn on soup maker and cook for 25 minutes on cook and blend setting
4. Add greek yogurt (optional) and pulse
5. Add more water if required

Time: 30 minutes
Amount: 4 servings

INGREDIENTS

- Carrots (5 medium)
- Leek (1, medium)
- Broccoli (1, small)
- Courgette (1/2 medium)
- Cauliflower (1, small)
- Parsley (1 tsp)
- Water
- Pepper and salt

HOW TO COOK

1	Clean and chop vegetables and add them to soup maker
2	Add water and seasoning then mix thoroughly
3	Turn on soup maker and blend-cook for about 25 minutes

THE ULTIMATE LEFTOVER VEGAN SOUP

NATIONAL CUISINE SOUP RECIPES

NATIONAL CUISINE SOUP RECIPES

CHINESE CHICKEN AND SWEETCORN SOUP

Time: 20 minutes

Amount: 4 servings

INGREDIENTS

- Uncooked sweetcorn (320g/11.3oz)
- Red onion (1, finely chopped)
- Cooked chicken (250g/9oz) shredded
- Water chestnuts (100g/3.5oz) thinly sliced
- Fresh ginger (1 tsp)
- Chicken stock (750 ml)
- Corn flour (2tsp) mixed with water (1 tsp) to form paste
- 4 spring onions (finely chopped)
- Red chilli pepper (seeds removed and finely chopped
- Coriander (10g)
- Cooked noodles (200g/7oz)

HOW TO MAKE

1. Pour chicken stock, sweetcorn kennel and red onion into soup maker along with water chestnut, red onion, shredded chicken, ginger and corn flour paste

2. Mix all ingredients thoroughly using a spoon.

3. Turn on soup maker and process on chunky mode

4. Divide cooked noodles between serving bowls, add chilli, coriander and spring onions then pour soup over noddles then serve.

Time: 30 minutes

Amount: 4 servings

INGREDIENTS

- Onion (5 large)
- Carrots (3 large)
- Celery (5 large sticks)
- Greek Yogurt (2 tbsp)
- Chives (2 tsp)
- Water (250 ml)
- Mixed herbs (1 tsp)
- Pepper and salt (to taste)
- Thyme (1 tsp)

HOW TO COOK

1	Dice the onions, celery and carrots
2	Pour all into the soup maker, add seasoning and some water
3	Pour in the greek yogurt
4	Cook for about 24 minutes on chunky setting

FRENCH ONION SOUP

THE ULTIMATE MEDITERRANEAN VEGETABLE SOUP

Time: 35 minutes

Amount: 4 servings

INGREDIENTS

- Onion (2 large)
- Red pepper (1 small)
- Green beans (100g/3.5oz)
- Leek (1 large)
- Carrots (5, large)
- Peeled potato (1, large)
- Sweet potato (1 small)
- Tinned tomatoes (1 can)
- Water (50ml)
- Oregano (1 tbsp)
- Chives (1 tsp)
- Garlic puree (2 tsp)
- Thyme (1 tsp)
- Soft cheese garlic & herb flavour (2 tbsp)

HOW TO COOK

1. Chop vegetables into small bite-sized chunks and place them in soup maker

2. Add tinned tomatoes and a little bit of water if necessary

3. Add seasoning

4. Cook in soup maker on regular cook setting for about 25 minutes without blending or in chunky mode.

5. Stir in soft cheese then serve.

CREAMY MOROCCAN CARROT SOUP

Time: 40 minutes

Amount: 4 servings

INGREDIENTS

- Carrots (12, large)
- Onion (1 large)
- Red pepper (1)
- Coconut milk (1 can)
- Garlic puree (2tsp)
- Water (100 ml)
- Cinnamon (1 tsp)
- Turmeric (1 tsp)
- Cuber ginger (peeled & grated)
- Coriander (2 tbsp)
- Pepper and salt

HOW TO COOK

1	Peel and dice onions, red pepper and carrots
2	Place all into soup maker
3	Add ginger, garlic and some other seasonings
4	Add coconut milk and some more water.
5	Pour in coconut milk and add more water.
6	Cook on blender the cook and bender feature and serve when ready.

THAI VEGETABLE CURRY

Time: 30 minutes

Amount: 5 servings

INGREDIENTS

- Leek (1 medium)
- Carrots (3 large)
- Courgette (1 small)
- Pumpkin (peeled & diced)
- Coconut milk (1 can)
- Thai curry paste (1 tsp)
- Garlic puree (1 tsp)
- Red pepper (1 small)
- Mustard (1 tsp)
- Paprika (2 tsp)
- Coriander (1 tsp)
- Mixed spice (1 tsp)
- Water (100ml)
- Pepper & salt

HOW TO COOK

1. Peel carrots, dice leek, and prepare red pepper and courgette
2. Place all vegetables in soup maker, add water and coconut milk then add seasoning
3. Cook in soup maker on chunky option for 25 minutes
4. Serve when ready. Can be served with crusty bread.

PORTUGUESE FISH SOUP

Time: 30 minutes

Amount: 4 servings

INGREDIENTS

- Carrot (1, large)
- Potatoes (2 medium)
- Red pepper (1, small)
- White fish (100g/3.5oz)
- Cams (a handful)
- Tinned tomatoes (1 can)
- Prawns (a handful)
- Red wine (1/3 cup)
- Garlic puree (2 tsp)
- Mustard (1 tsp)
- Paprika (2 tsp)
- Water
- Pepper and salt

HOW TO MAKE

1. Clean, peel and chop potatoes and carrot
2. Dice white fish and red pepper, put all into soup maker
3. Add seafood to the maker.
4. Add the wine, potatoes and seasoning.
5. Turn on soup maker and mix well on chunky setting for 25 minutes
6. You can serve soup with warm crusty bread. You can also add a sprinkle of thyme on top.

EASY INDIAN PRAWN SOUP

Time: 35 minutes

Amount: 4 servings

INGREDIENTS

- Fresh prawns (2 kg/4.5kg)
- Red pepper (1 red)
- 1 onion (small)
- Coriander (3 tsp)
- Curry powder (4 tsp)
- Mixed spice (1 tsp)
- Ginger puree (2 tsp)
- Lime juice & rind
- Greek yogurt (4 tbsp)
- Fish stock (100ml)
- Pepper and salt to taste

HOW TO COOK

1	Peel onion then dice. Do the same for red pepper
2	Put both in the soup maker
3	Remove shell from prawns and place them in the soup maker
4	Add spices and pour in fish stock. Blend in soup maker for about 25 minutes
5	Add Greek yogurt and lime then pulse soup maker.

GAZPACHO

Time: 12 hours 20 minutes
Amount: 4 servings

INGREDIENTS

- 18 tomatoes
- Cucumbers (2, diced)
- Red pepper (2, chopped)
- Garlic (5 clove, chopped)
- 3/4 baguette (cut into smaller bits)
- Wine vinegar (7 tbs)
- Pepper and salt (added to taste)
- Olive oil (5 tbsp)
- Tabasco (1tbsp)
- Cucumber julienne-garnish

HOW TO COOK

1. Mix all the ingredients (except oil) in a bowl. Cover & leave in a refrigerator for about 12 hours to marinate.

2. Transfer to soup maker and blend soup. Add seasoning as desired

3. Serve soup in bowls & garnish with cucumber julienne and the extra virgin olive oil

CHINESE EASY HOT AND SOUR SOUP

Time: **30 minutes**

Amount:**1 or 2 servings**

INGREDIENTS

- Low-salt chicken broth (1 litre)
- Marinated and sauted pork loin (1/2 lb/0.3kg)
- Chinese chili bean paste (toban djan)- 3 tbsp
- Rice vinegar (3 tbsp)
- Wood ear mushrooms (4)
- Shimeji mushroom (about 1 cup)
- Cornstarch (1.5 tbsp)
- Form tofu (in cubes, 1 cup)
- Egg (1 large)
- Shanghai noodles (4 oz/113g)

HOW TO COOK

1. Rehydrate wood ear mushrooms by soaking it in boiling water for 30 minutes or more before you begin cooking. You can wrap the hydrated mushrooms in a damp paper towel

2. Add chicken broth, chilli paste, vinegar and small slices of chop wood ear mushroom in a soup maker. Also add the shimeji mushrooms, corn starch, tofu and pork cook in a soup maker for 24 minutes.

3. Open soup maker and add whisked egg to the soup in a slow thin stream. Cook without blending for some minutes more

4. Can be served with Shanghai noddles

ITALIAN WEDDING SOUP

Time: 35 minutes

Amount: 8 servings

INGREDIENTS

- Meatballs
- low sodium chicken broth (12 cups)
- Curly endive or escarole (1 lb/0.45kg)- coarsely chopped
- Eggs (2, large)
- Parmesan (freshly grated, 2 tbsp)- plus more for garnish
- Fresh ground black pepper
- Salt

HOW TO COOK

1. Place meatballs and the curly endive into soupmaker and cook for about 10 minutes

2. While it cooks, whisk eggs & cheese in a medium bowl.

3. Drizzle egg mixture into the broth stirring gently as you do so.

4. Add pepper & salt as desired

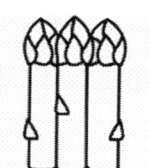

The opinions and ideas of the author contained in this publication are designed to educate the reader in an informative and helpful manner. While we accept that the instructions will not suit every reader, it is only to be expected that the recipes might not gel with everyone. Use the book responsibly and at your own risk. This work with all its contents, does not guarantee correctness, completion, quality or correctness of the provided information. Always check with your medical practitioner should you be unsure whether to follow a low carb eating plan. Misinformation or misprints cannot be completely eliminated. Human error is real!

Picture: Foxys Forest Manufacture // shutterstock.com

Design: Oliviaprodesign

Printed in Great Britain
by Amazon